The Bradford Poems

Acknowledgements

Some of these poems have appeared in the following publications: *The New Statesman*, *The Spectator*, *The Oldie* and in the collections *Bradford and Beyond* (Flambard Press) and *A Good Time* (smith|doorstop).

Thanks also to Jan Huntley for the author photo on the back cover and for her kindness and help at various stages in putting this book together.

Many thanks to Peter and Gillian Hill for their friendship and support throughout Gerard's illness. Gerard knew that, thanks to them, this book was in production, and it moved him greatly. I add my gratitude to his. CB

The Bradford Poems
Gerard Benson

smith|doorstop

Published 2014 by
smith|doorstop Books
The Poetry Business
Bank Street Arts
32-40 Bank Street
Sheffield S1 2DS
www.poetrybusiness.co.uk

Copyright © The estate of Gerard Benson 2014

ISBN 978-1-910367-35-3

The estate of Gerard Benson hereby asserts the moral right to be identified as the author of this book.

British Library Cataloguing-in-Publication Data.
A catalogue record for this book is available from the
British Library.

Typeset by Utter
Printed by Printondemand.com
Cover photo by kind permission of Dean Smith of Camera Crew
www.cameracrewphoto.co.uk
Cover author photo: Jan Huntley

smith|doorstop is a member of Inpress,
www.inpressbooks.co.uk. Distributed by Central Books Ltd.,
99 Wallis Road, London E9 5LN.

The Poetry Business is an Arts Council
National Portfolio Organisation

Supported by
ARTS COUNCIL ENGLAND

Contents

8   Foreword
9   Ballad of the Cliffe Wood Boar

Commisioned

14 In Commemoration of the Bradford City Fire –
    11th May 1985
15 Untold Stories
17 Speaking Up
18 Veterans' Day
19 Armistice Bird
20 The Scientists
22 Soundtrack For Bradford film poem
24 Sports Centre
25 St Patrick's Night
27 Fugue at St. Georges
28 On Being Appointed Bradford's Poet Laureate

Charities

30 Alzheimer's
31 Teddies!
33 Spring Fayre
34 A Reet Good Yorkshire Lunch
35 Calypso
36 Farewell

Calendar Poems

40 January
41 February
42 March
43 April

44 May
45 June
46 July
47 August
48 September
49 October
50 November
51 December

Bradford Poems

54 In Praise of Yorkshire
55 Interchange Bus Station at Night
57 Snapshot: Interchange Bus Station
58 Les Parapluies de Bradford
59 Morning Scene in Ashwell Road
60 City Park
61 Haworth
62 Undercliffe
64 Galleries
65 Saltaire Festival
67 Joan Armatrading at St. George's Hall
68 Bradford Brevities, 1
69 Bradford Brevities, 2
70 Chosen
71 Rubai for Mr Hafeez Johar
72 I, too, can write a Ghazal if I try
74 Garlic
75 Winter Stew
76 So Snow
77 Eclipse
78 If I Hadn't Been a Writer
80 How Delightful To Know Mr Benson
81 Community Pride

To Gerard's many friends in Bradford, and the people he met as Poet Laureate, and particularly to the former Lord Mayor and Lady Mayoress who made possible the publication of this book, Peter and Gillian Hill.

Foreword

Although an 'Off cum'd 'un', Gerard Benson became a much loved honorary Bradfordian during his time as Poet Laureate for the City, an affection that Gerard returned in full measure. His wit, pin sharp observation and great ability with words resulted in this book of poems, on and about the diverse peoples that make up our city.

As Poet Laureate from 2008, Lord Mayors of Bradford have enjoyed his ability to encapsulate their charitable aims in verse. These were always right to the point, often touched with gentle humour and sometimes requested at short notice!

Sadly, Gerard's passing in April 2014, after a long battle with cancer, has left his friends, family and our city, much the poorer.

Respected as he was as our Poet Laureate, many are unaware that here was a man of great stature with a national reputation as an author, performer and teacher in the worlds of poetry, theatre and music, as well as the co-founder of Poems on the Underground, which still flourishes today.

On a personal note, we first met Gerard and his wife Cathy in May 2010 and from being colleagues they soon became good friends. In the last year of his life Gerard put together this collection, but sadly he did not survive to see it published. It is with great pleasure that we are able to fulfil one of his last wishes and bring you this book of poems dedicated to the people of Bradford.

Peter & Gill

Ballad of the Cliffe Wood Boar

A mile to the north of Bradford Church
   A small oak forest stood,
The dangerous haunt of boars and wolves,
   Which people called Cliffe Wood.

And there, there dwelt a mighty boar,
   A huge ferocious beast,
A massive tusker, weighing, oh,
   Three hundredweight at least.

He ravaged all the country round
   And terrified the folk;
And none dared drink at Cliffe Wood well
   Beside the parish oak.

For there the wild boar used to drink
   And no-one dared go near,
His razor tusks! His lightning speed!
   They held their lives too dear.

The cattle, too, he terrified,
   The sheep and the forest deer –
And so the village of Bradford
   Became a place of fear.

Then spoke the Lord of Manor Court,
   His voice both loud and sure:
"I will reward the man or youth
   Who'll rid us of this boar."

"I will reward the hunter,"
   The Lord of the Manor said,
"Who'll free us from this menacing beast,
   And bring it to me, dead.

"He will become a wealthy man,
   This creature plagues us so."
Then young John Northrop sallied forth
   And cut him self a bow.

He sharpened three good arrows
   And went out to Cliffe Wood
To seek the ravening monster
   And slay him if he could.

To slay the ravening monster
   Or he, himself be slain.
He waited a while by Cliffe Wood well
   And did not wait in vain.

For when the wild boar came to drink
   And bent his head down low,
John took a feathered arrow
   And strung it to his bow.

His good yew bow he steadied
   And loosed the fateful dart,
Straight at the drinking creature
   And pierced him through the heart.

Then, with the well-honed dagger
   Which from his baldrick hung
He sliced from out of the cruel mouth
   The creature's slavered tongue.

Now the forest was a hiding place
   For men beyond the law
And one of them, out hunting, found
   The corpse of the Cliffe Wood boar.

He knew of the reward and thought
   "If I cut off this head,
And take it off to Manor Court
   To prove the beast is dead,
I'll get the reward instead, I will.
   I'll get the reward instead."

So off he ran to Manor Court
   And stood before the Lord
And swore he'd killed the Cliffe Wood boar,
   Swore by St. Peter's sword.

But when they opened that fearsome mouth
   They found no tongue inside,
Which took the villain by surprise;
   And then they knew he'd lied.

Just then John Northrop hurried in,
   So handsome and so young,
With his bow and arrows slung on his back,
   Bearing the creature's tongue.

This was the proof. He'd killed the beast,
   And so gained the reward –
A plot of land up Horton way
   Donated by my Lord;

John's and his family's for all time –
   For some as yet unborn,
But they must, on St. Martin's Day
   Give three blasts on a horn.

This happened many years ago,
   Six hundred years or more,
But now surmounting the Bradford Arms
   You can see the head of a boar,
Above the Bradford Shield of Arms,
   The tongueless head of a boar.

Commisioned

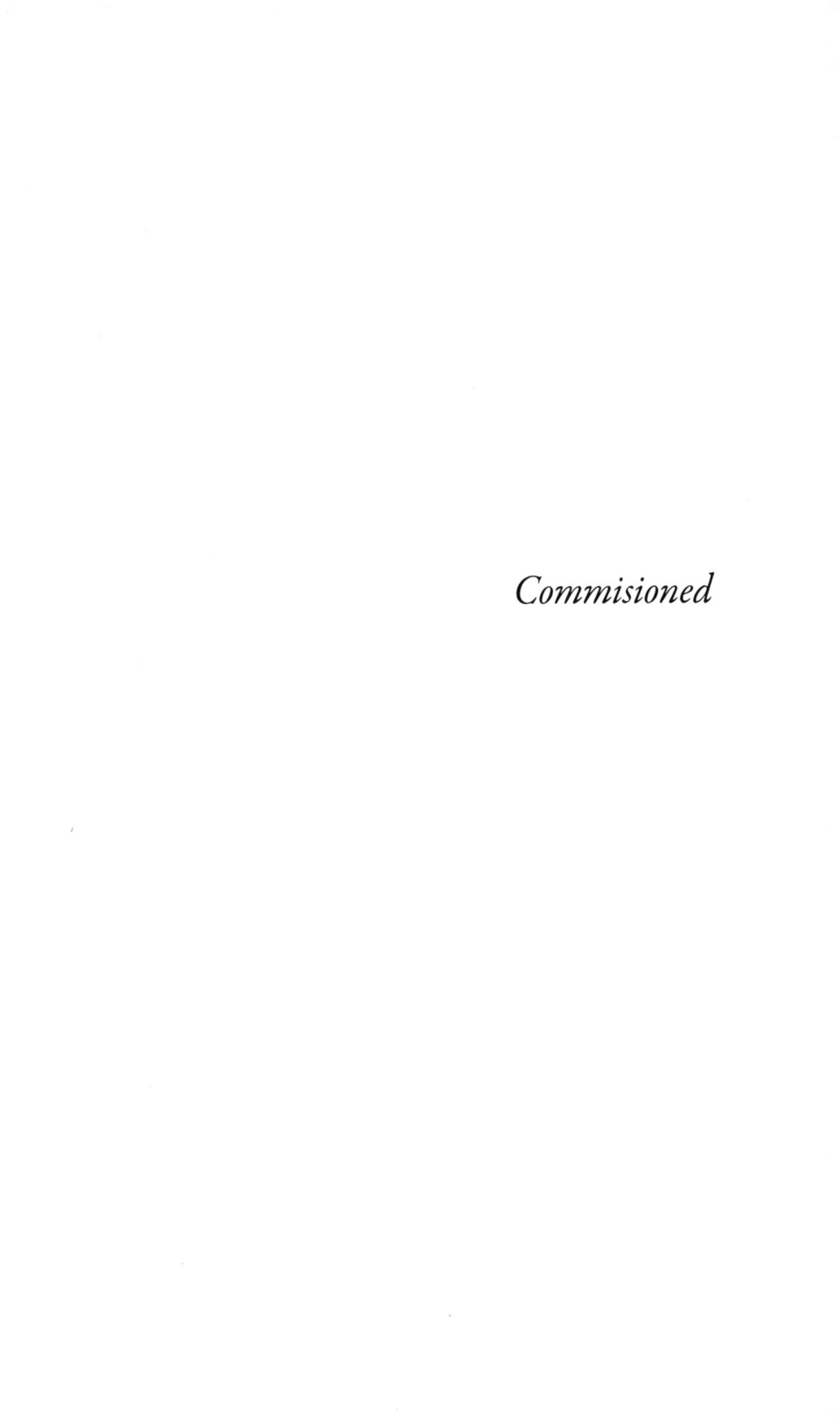

In Commemoration of the Bradford City Fire – 11th May 1985

The scrambling over barriers, the rampaging flames,
That dog-end, the huge black cloud, the abandoned game.
    We must remember these ...
The cameras which watched while the flames soared.
The grieving city. The lost lives. The injured. The scared.
    We must remember.

There is human bravery too, to commemorate:
The quick-thinking men who smashed down the locked gate
    We remember.
The courage of police and public; the rescues deserve praise.
The escorting of injured people while the fire blazed
    We remember too.

But gathered now on this tragic anniversary
We pray for the healing of our community.
    Though the pain is remembered,
We've had support from friends world-wide
Helping us to change, rebuild community pride.
    This, too, we shall remember.

Untold Stories
A Poem for Holocaust Memorial Day 2011

Let there be no more holocausts,
   No more brutal solutions.
No more fear of the knock on the door.
   Let there be Peace between peoples,
      Peace between nations.

Let there be no more round-ups
   Nor terror on railway stations,
No more fear of the prowling car.
   Let there be Peace between peoples,
      Peace between nations.

There are so many untold holocaust stories
So many holocausts. Where does one begin?
   The Tattooed Number. The Child's violin.
   The Halted Train. The Visa in the Bin.
   The Hunted Hunter. The Compassionate Guard.
   The Field of Turnips. The Identity Card.
   The African Tree. The Abattoir.
   The Stolen Wheelchair. The Painted Star.
   The Shattered Door. The Broken Code.
   The Never-come Day. The Endless Road.
     So many untold stories,
     Terrifying but true.
     These are merely the titles;
     The stories I leave to you.

Let there be no more genocide,
   No more sour suspicion,
No more fear of the ice-cold stare.
   There must be Peace between peoples,
      Peace between nations;
   Peace between whole peoples
      And Love between nations.

Speaking Up
A Poem for Holocaust Memorial Day 2012

When the fellow in the café tells a subtly racist joke
   And the people sitting round him laugh or smile,
Do I join in with the laughter, like all the other folk,
   Or do I let them know I think it's vile?
     If I don't speak up, who will?

When a homophobic oaf decides to pick on some poor guy,
   And others, half in jest, also deride,
Do you go with the majority, or do you ask him why
   He's so sure he's got the people on his side?
     If you don't speak up, who will?

For it often starts in small ways with a gesture or remark
   Quite what is going on we don't enquire;
But these minuscule beginnings can light a little spark
   That will grow into a wildly raging fire.
     If we don't speak up, who will?

With niggles and with nudges persecution can begin.
   With dehumanising language it continues,
Till a holocaust has happened, where once decent folk had been,
   With the systematic murder of the Jews.
     Why did no-one speak up, no-one speak out
       Against that yellow star?
       Things had gone too far.

       Speak up, speak out,
       If I don't, you don't, we don't..
       Then who will?

Veterans' Day

It's big band numbers in Centenary Square,
and a few fellows watching, or stepping, forties fashion,
with women in their arms, I think their hair
might well displease their old sergeant-majors –
and as to its colour, well it's white or at least grey.
Or absent. Some are in old uniforms, rather too large,
or mock-ups. Their shoes are well-polished. But, hey!
that man's in trainers, Sergeant. Put him on a charge.

A swing band plays Glenn Miller arrangements
But they're easy on that military precision.
It's 2008. There's a sense of estrangement
from the past – those stringent war-time conditions.
   It's a cheerful scene, with comradeship. It feels good.
   They shuffle, foxtrot, even jive. They're In the Mood.

Armistice Bird

After the cannonades, after the bayonet charges,
After the digging of trenches and latrines,
After the long exhausting forced marches
After the agonising station farewell scenes;

After the letters home, after the infestations,
After the civvies and the parlyvoo,
After the destruction, after the devastation,
After the dreams of demons coming at you;

After the slaughter, after the groaning on the wire,
After the ceremonial battlefield Mass,
After the terrifying machine gun fire,
After the howling shells, after the mustard gas;

After the unending clamour of war,
In that eleventh month, after the violence,
On that eleventh day at the eleventh hour,
There came at last a silence. A healing silence.

And men in filthy boots, and bereaved women
In farmhouse lofts, listened with ears rinsed clean.
And someone, somewhere, heard a songbird singing,
Singing out hope in a world become sane again.

The Scientists

The man in the cave mouth
Looked up at the stars.
So bright, So many. So strangely patterned.
Not there during the day.
He watched as they wheeled round the sky
as the seasons slowly changed,
began to wonder why. How? and why?

The woman on the grassy ledge
watched the river
as it bubbled over pebbles,
how it tumbled when it reached an edge,
how it broadened and moved more slowly,
how it seemed to have a skin,
how there was always more water from the sky.
She wondered how and why.

Scientific thinkers whose names are unknown.
One realised you could see the time
in the length of the shadows,
one saw that round things rolled,
another that wild dogs fear the fire,
that trees lose their leaves then live again.
They looked at the sky
the sun sailed across it daily,
the moon changed shape nightly,
sometimes you could see it in the daytime.
They wanted to know why. How and why.

White-coated now in labs and universities
they perform experiments, publish their theories,
in direct line from those enquiring ancestors
who looked at water and the sky

and creatures and plants,
and began to figure how and why.

What do we say to our children
when they want to know why ice melts
or how bees make honey,
or what happens when you mix this with that,
or why hair grows and doesn't hurt if you cut it?
What do we offer
when they want to know how and why?

Soundtrack For Bradford film poem

Peace Museum, Peace Studies, Peace Trail, Parks.
Real mixing of cultures in John Street Market.
International provisions. Integrated communities.
Drugs, feuds, crime, you may read about .... BUT
Everywhere you'll find ordinary folk, working, living together.

❊

In this house lived three amazing sisters,
And in this village street the stones they trod.
And in this dark church graveyard
Stones engraved with the names and dates
Of children killed by cholera.
And over these windswept moors strode Heathcliff
Calling, calling for his Catherine.

❊

Here Dickens read to an audience of thousands
And Doddy did his diddy jokes.
A living seat of history.
Oistrach played here; Joan Armatrading sang,
Brass bands have oompahed, and dancers whirled.
Name it, you've probably heard it here.

❊

How we used to live.
How we used to work.
The kitchens we had. The old range ovens.
The machines, Looms. Carding machines in a mill town,
And maintained by the breweries,
The handsome great dray horses.

❋

In this museum with its three cinema screens
Everything you wished to know about photography.
This is Bradford, City of Film. Camera Obscura.
Brownies, Kodaks. Television Cameras. Strange mirrors.
All here for you to play with.

❋

A multi-mix city
With melas
And busy people;
With lively children
And in the winter months,
Christmas, Eid and Diwali
Up in lights!

Sports Centre
(B Active)

Ann said, "Are you going to write a poem about us?"
We'd been bending and stretching together in Susan's class:

Toe-taps, and half-stars; dumbbells, stability balls (don't ask!)
Squats, sidesteps, shoulder-rolls (and other more taxing tasks),

In track suits and trainers and printed tee-shirts
We bend this way and that, till it almost hurts.

(Who said "almost"?) "You could call it," Ann said
"The Geriatric Gymnasts." But I've been racking my head.

And I've got a better idea than that. And the drift is
Something like this: "The Fit and Feisty Over-Fifties."

St Patrick's Night

At Bradford's fine college,
The Fount of all Knowledge,
Meself got an invite to party a bit
There was everyone there,
From the Cook to the Mayor.
(I *should* say the *Lord* Mayor. It just wouldn't fit.)

'Twas a marvellous Hall
With pillars and all
And plentiful tables to sit us all down.
And the dinner we ate,
Och, boys, it was great,
'Twas surely the best to be had in the Town.

I doubt if the Salmon
Was pulled from the Shannon,
'Twas tasty enough, for all that, I declare.
And the Dogsbody Band
Was exceedingly grand
Whether playing for Dancing or Singing an Air.

And as for the dancing:
Think jigging and prancing,
And shuffling and kicking (and bumping besides),
And puffing and blowing,
And coming and going,
And swinging of partners and changing of sides.

Then after a Waltz
    We played "True or False?"
In aid of Alzheimer's, we each paid a fee
    And wouldn't you know it?
    'Twas won by a poet!
The brain* of that fella's a marvel to see.

    But midnight approaches
    'Tis time for our coaches.
St Patrick's been honoured. It's time to depart.
    All things must be ended
    No matter how splendid
So home we all wend with a good happy heart.

*Instead of "brain" the original read "luck"; clearly a typing error.

Fugue at St. Georges

torn-off
   scraps of tune
  chase
    one another

twist
    and manoeuvre
   through the vast maze
of C major

  as intricate
    and complex
   a code
as enigma

attain
  a final chord
end triumphantly
   together

On Being Appointed Bradford's Poet Laureate

How can I find a rhyme for Bradford?
I can't even remember what I had for d
inner.
My inner
peace is quite undone;
now if it had been London
I could have manage
d, or even at a pinch Swanage.
If it had been Rye
I'd have given it a try,
Crewe,
and I'd have known what to do –
Newcastle-on-Tyne
Would have suited me fine,
Or even
Steven
age or Edin-
burgh or Reading.

But trying to find a rhyme for Bradford
Has been driving me mad for d
ays.
I'll probably be had for d
eception or false pretences, (though
pretences are by their nature false, you know).
If it had been Baildon
I wouldn't have failed 'em,
But Bradford! I'd be glad for d
emonstration that I'm wrong
but I'm convinced it can't be done.

Charities

Alzheimer's

Yes, he said with a doleful grin, *I've got Alpiner's Disease.*
I saw an empty landscape, featureless, white,
and my old friend, precarious on skis
travelling rapidly downward, vanishing from sight.

I kept my thoughts to myself and smiled back.
I know who you are he said, *but I've forgot*
it's on the tip of my ... he floundered and lost track
and gazed through me, seeing who knows what.

Alzheimer's is a strange disease, inexorable, cruel.
It steals a person's inner core. Their selfhood goes.
There was Joe in my group at the London Hospital,
he stroked the table while he sang a little phrase:

the same snatch all day: *di-di-di-dum-dum.*
"You used to be a tailor, weren't you Joe?"
said the thoughtful therapist. *Di-di-di-dum-dum;*
I don't know what I was. I don't know.

(Shocking words.) And Penelope, puzzled, imploring:
I can feel it going away from me. Can you
help me? Help me before I lose everything!
She grabbed my sleeve, but what could I do?

I think about Margaret, who'd forgotten how to eat;
the food spooned into her mouth just stayed there,
and Bridget, my aunt, who'd made me a bit of a favourite
and now greeted me with a stranger's stare.

My old friend said, smiling, *I've got Alpiner's Disease*
and I saw an empty landscape, hospital white
and my friend firmly buckled onto waxed skis
plunging rapidly downward, vanishing from sight.

Teddies!

From the two ends of the field we came,
   A thousand kids and more,
And formed a massive circle round
   Like the tail of a dinosaur.

And everyone held a Teddy
   Or a different soft toy,
A thousand or more little cuddlies,
   One for each girl and boy.

There were tigers and lions and leopards
   A sheep and a kangaroo,
Ducks and geese and elephants
   And even a dolly or two.

There were shreks and elves and clowns,
   A Goldilocks saying her prayers,
A floppy giraffe that would make you laugh,
   But mostly they were bears.

Yes, mostly they were Teddies
   Of various shapes and sizes,
Some wore skirts and some wore nowt
   And some wore tops and trousers.

There were grown-ups there as well,
   Each with a toy or a bear,
Teachers and helpers and dinner ladies,
   And of course our own Lord Mayor.

When the signal was given
  We all held hands and toys,
And stood there for a minute –
  A thousand girls and boys.

Well, a good deal more than a thousand
  I like to get these things straight,
Including all the grown-ups
  Two thousand and two-fifty-eight.

And then we gave three great cheers.
  You could hear them for miles around
I bet that part of Bradford
  Has never heard such a sound.

It was all to help Little Heroes
  Kids with a nasty disease,
But we had lots of fun doing it
  In spite of the sharp south breeze.

And so we broke a World Record,
  Kids from two Bradford schools,
And here's what we learnt that day:
  Caring for others rules, OK?
  Caring for others rules!

Spring Fayre

Roll up! Roll up for the Springtime Fayre!
What will you buy? Something to wear?
A scarf for your neck? A comb for your hair?
What will you buy at the Springtime Fayre.

What will you get at the Springtime Fayre?
A toy for the kids? A nice teddy bear?
Or a comfy new cushion for that armchair?
Roll up! Roll up to the Springtime Fayre.

Whatever you buy at the Great Spring Fayre,
There are people in need, well everywhere,
Just spend a few pence here and there,
Or pounds, if you like if you really care.

Roll up to the Springtime Fayre!
What will you buy? Some new kitchenware?
You don't have to be a millionaire.
Roll up! Roll up to the Springtime Fayre!
Roll up to the Springtime Fayre!

A Reet Good Yorkshire Lunch

We're sat for a reet good Yorkshire lunch
'Cos we're a reet good Yorkshire bunch
    Tucking into t'grub,
In the Victoria Hotel
A place that suits uz very well
    'sbetter nor any pub.

There's our Lord Mayor and his good wife;
I wish them long and happy life
    And just a year of office;
And many another V.I.P.
A veritable company.
    We'll last through to the coffees.

But are we really all real tykes?
Did some of uz get on our bikes
    To gain this noble status.
Ours is not to reason why;
Ours is just to eat uz pie
    With or without potatoes.

The food is good, the company grand
You'll not find better in the land
    You'll not find any bores.
There's reet good folk from wall to wall,
Tykes or not tykes. And best of all
    It's all in a reet good cause.

It's all in a reet good cause indeed.
Our Lord Mayor knows what children need,
    So we've got him to thank.
He knows kids need creative play
That's why all uz support today
    That play place at Nell Bank.

Calypso

Our Lord Mayor
He really care
For those poor old-timers
Who've got that terr-
ible affair
They call Alzheimers.

He raise a fund
To help them on
So everyone
Come on
It's time now for some giving.
Show that you care
Like our Lord Mayor
What can you spare
To make their lives worth living?

Our Lord Mayor
He really care
For folk who've got Alzheimers;
So take your share
What can you spare
For those old-timers.

Farewell
(A western ghazal)

We've come today in this great house of prayer
to wish a last farewell to our Lord Mayor.

That time has come. We're sad to see her go;
it's been another rich and fruitful year.

We come today in this great house of prayer
to wish a last farewell to our Lord Mayor.

There was the opening of City Park
with dancing acrobats high in the air,

and children splashing in the fountain jets
and joyful people in the city square.

And yet it isn't just these grand affairs
that form life's fabric for a real Lord Mayor.

There are those hundreds of obscure events,
opening a nursery school, the Christmas Fayre.

youth club or dining club or old folks' home,
or Women's Day; or meetings she must chair.

Cancer research, the Marie Curie fund
she's worked for us tirelessly and with true flair.

We come today in this great house of prayer,
to wish a last farewell to our Lord Mayor.

She's earned a rest, after her busy year,
when she's been here and there and everywhere.

※

The time has come, you've really done your share
And now we wish a fond farewell, Lord Mayor.

Calendar Poems

January

Ice hangs from the roof
in dangerous daggers.
Our robin is fluffed up,
bold on the bird table.
Your breath is a cloud
floating by your face.
Trees are stark,
branches bare.

Ice hangs from the roof
in dangerous daggers.
Sounds are magnified;
the grinding of gears
is clearly heard
more than a mile away..
The evening sky
is weighted with weather..

February

Those days when after a week of heavy cloud
the sun comes up over the neighbours' roofs.
Taking peelings to the compost I hear the loud
shrill assertions of the garden's birds; grouped
in the trees they assault the ear with twittering song.
Green shoots here and there. And a fierce breeze
keeps the bushes in motion. The slow, long
winter nights are shorter now. Soon bees
will be flying in and out of the little hole
under the step – wasps, too, if we're unlucky.
It's too soon to shed a jumper but I'm on a roll;
it's bright today, gleaming. The paths are mucky
after the buckets of rain but the flags have a sheen,
dazzling the eye. And everywhere the promise of green.

March

Today it's racing clouds
And sparrows pecking on the path
like clockwork toys,
till a sleek wood pigeon

settles his bulk among them
and takes over the hovering,
and they, with one mind,
lift and regroup in a nearby bush.

There's a bite in the breeze
and the earth is still soaked
with yesterday's rain.
But everything's shining.

And look! Across the line
of quivering brown sticks
just touched with green
that are the garden trees

one white butterfly
is staggering through the air;
in the space of a second
seen and gone.

April

A plump crow in a blossoming cherry tree
stumbles and hops from twigs to branch, bobbing
the boughs. Clumsy. Lout in a lingerie
department. Insolent border guard, grubbing
through intimate belongings, thick thumbs
and gloved fingers shifting papers and clothing
and toilet preparations. So April comes
with a cold wind and ragged clouds scooting
over a pale sky, with washing blown out straight,
shirtsleeves reaching for the horizon. The crow
lumps his way through, hustling his weight
about, scuffing the bright petalled snow –
a dozen brush-strokes of shiny black paint –
opens his dark bill, gives voice, a harsh complaint.

May

For just a day or two, the peonies,
wonderful fists of deep red petals, adorn
the gardens; and in woods, under the trees,
bluebells work their strange magic; one lawn
I pass has buttercups and sharp-eyed daisies.
Over another, dandelions have rampaged,
shown their fabulous blond heads, greyed,
then gone bald and spread their flat green leaves.
Everywhere I look there's green. Weeds
burgeon, dock and ladies' mantle, couch grass,
enchanters' nightshade. We have warm days
then sudden showers and even bursts of hail.
But for today the sky is blue, no cloud.
There's a wind, though, bashing the bushes about.

June

Sweet honeysuckle and the symphonies of birds
whistling and counterwhistling in the wood.
Weeds colonise the garden. I feel the words
of a song busting out all over. I could
linger a long time in this burgeoning;
loving and hating the dandelions and bellbind,
their persistence, the assertive power they bring
with their beautiful flowers – one splendid,
a rival sun, the other, insidious, tendrilled,
white, lovely. I see foxgloves, pansies, roses.
Two tail-swishing horses in a farmer's field;
a child in jeans caresses their soft noses,
feeding them apples by a five-bar gate.
And I can hear June's dubious double note.

July

Hot feet in sandals. And far away
down the road, those pools of clear
water which vanish as you draw near.
A shimmer over the baked pathway
distorts the grass stems, wobbles the air.

Children shelter from the sun.
Butterflies. Bird song. Dry lawns.
Peeled skin. Bushes turn brown.
Deck chair. Cool drink. Sun hat.
Long cotton dresses. Sleepless nights.

August

I'm sitting in a deck chair, having a little think,
and idly watching two huge dragon flies,
and wondering who will bring me a nice long cool drink.

I've left the washing up in the kitchen sink.
The kids are out playing; I can hear their distant cries.
I'm sitting in a deck chair having a little think.

From my neighbour's garden I can hear that icy clink;
I see his loaded tray with envious eyes,
and wonder: Might *he* offer me a nice long cool drink?

My skin is slowly turning a horrid shade of pink
but it's far too much bother to shift or rise.
I'm sitting in a deck chair having a little think.

Ask me what I'm thinking. I'll tell you with a wink.
And when you hear my answer it'll come as no surprise.
I'm thinking: Who will bring me a nice long cool drink?

I'm too lazy to move, can't even be bothered to blink.
I'm waiting for a breeze and studying the skies,
lolling in my deck chair, having a little think,
and wondering who will bring me a nice long cold cold drink.

September

The year's moving on. It's not imperceptible
if you watch for it. Every line of trees
has its maverick. By minute degrees
the green is being subverted by subtle
faint yellows and rusty browns, the odd scribble
of tangerine is beginning to show; every breeze
collects a few more hostages; and these
day-to-day changes are quite visible
if you stay alert. But if you glance away
it all happens without you. I can remember
years when the seasons simply rolled by,
undercranked, a film speeded up: spring flowers,
roses, chrysanthemums. And suddenly December –
stripped trees, frosty breath, dark hours.

October
(High wind in Queensbury)

Up on this height you can hear the roar and hurl of it,
and see early fallen leaves racing across gardens,
flying about the streets, suddenly alive again.
The trees are thrashing their wooden arms
and bunches of foraging starlings flutter sideways.

Clinging to their hats or chasing them, coats flapping
people struggle to work, rocked back from time to time.
A clattering hubcap rolls and smashes against a van.
Shawls fly up in calligraphic curves. But the clouds
have gone, that dark weight that loomed all week.

High in the trees plastic bags writhe, tormented ghosts.
Tights freed from a washing line are trapped in a rose bush.
There are branches in the road, a fallen wheelie bin.
Doors heave at their hinges; windows rattle their frames.
And listen. The chimneys are playing their sinister music.

November

The big beeches spread their diminishing systems
upward, black nets which trawl the darkening air,
or vein and artery charts sketched on the western
skyline, or templates for brains; they loom there
powerful with unintended meaning, this winter nightfall:
bough, branch and twig. How do I now
even imagine high summer, delightful
in succulent green, or autumn's umber show?
Bough and branch and twig; they're blacker than
the dusty city sky: and high up, hunched
like a pack of knives, a crow silhouette. It's afternoon,
just four o'clock. A fog is forming. Fists bunched
into deep overcoat pockets, I watch my breath
winding into the fog, inches from my mouth.

December

A long flat wooden shovel in my hands
(like a For Sale sign uprooted and turned over)
I push aside the heavy snow to uncover
the hidden pathway. These are not large grounds,
just forty yards from door to gate, but it sends
the blood pumping hard, this chilly endeavour,
shifting the insistent cold invader, which never
lets up in its sly campaign, occupying as it lands,
concealing all traces. The gardens look curiously
peaceful, content under the stifling,
anaesthetic snow, which soothes, most patiently,
all fractures. And while my neighbour is levelling
his pathway I see his dark cap gradually
whitening. 'Lots more up there,' he says, still shovelling.

Bradford Poems

In Praise of Yorkshire

Mills and minsters, worshippers, workers,
and a sense of generations, here, then gone,
of ordinary folk, clogging along
in the streets and lanes of Yorkshire.

The Dales, cricket, rhubarb, Delius,
Hutton, Hockney, Hughes and Auden.
The wildlife centres, the nature gardens:
A lot to be proud of in Yorkshire.

Sister novelists whose work survived it all,
Caedmon of Whitby's simple prayer,
that spooky jolly song, *On Ilkla Moor*,
still sung, not just in Yorkshire.

Butted onto the cold North Sea.
Flanked by the backbone Pennines;
Spread into thirdings, the Ridings.
Yorkshire. That's our Yorkshire.

Interchange Bus Station at Night

Stand at one end
and it's a lesson in perspective.
The orderly lines –
lights, floor markings,
glass panels, seats, bins,
all narrow away from you,
race toward an imagined point
infinitely distant.

And the people,
a hundred at least
scattered around:
though they are smaller
as they recede
into the distance,
their heads
are at the same level.

Anoraks, hoods, track suits,
shalwar kameez, sarees,
jeans, overcoats, trilbies,
baseball caps,
slim-heeled boots with pointed toes,
scuffed trainers, buffed brogues;
so various, the people
waiting by the lettered stands.

Four teenage girls, giggling;
rowdy football fans, old couple,
man staggering, beer-can in hand,
high-visibility man, glaring yellow;
glass, neat metal seating,
all vanishing
along converging lines
into the infinite distance.

Snapshot: Interchange Bus Station

Watched by a matching pair
of chatting mums,
three little girls,
up late,

way past their bed-time,
are dancing,
using the floor's pattern
for choreographic inspiration.

Feet moving,
arms gesturing,
gravely concentrating,
they move to an inner music.

Les Parapluies de Bradford

Bradford is a city with a wealth of umbrellas;
the ladies have them, and so do the fellas.

You see them in the streets and in the parks;
you even see them at the melas.

Some flourish them as they walk along,
some spin them like propellers.

You see them all – the patterned ones,
the blacks, the reds, the yellers.

I haven't got one of my own
but sometimes borrow Isabella's.

They're fairly useless in deserts and such
but a must for Pennine city dwellers.

Mary Poppins made good use of hers;
they're a Godsend to novelists and story tellers.

When they blow inside out they are abandoned;
you see their skeletons in gutters or stuck in a trellis.

I don't remember any brollies in fairy stories,
your Three Bearses and your Cinderellas,

possibly because they hadn't been invented
when the stories were written, as well as

the fact that they lack romance. But in Bradford
as I said before there are plenty of umbrellas.

Morning Scene in Ashwell Road

The morning is clean and cold; there's a frost on the grass,
and etchings of ice on the telephone kiosk's glass.

A handsome woman in a gold shalwar kameez
walks through her breath under the trees.

The air is still; and sounds are sharp and clear,
from over a mile away I can hear

the City Hall clock smack out the time.
A thin man with a stick limps through the rime.

A gesticulating lady with a mobile phone
communicates with a person or persons unknown

outside the door of the doctor's surgery,
then seeing me walk towards it, races me

to get inside first. Above, many white clouds flock
serenely westward. It has just struck ten o'clock.

Nobody smashed up the telephone kiosk last night –
pray God the local vandals are alright.

City Park

Water drops in sunshine
glint like cut glass.

Children shout
and play in the water.

City Hall
admires its reflection.

Fountains spring
to strange heights.

Children splash
playing with diamonds.

All's right with the world
in Bradford's City Park.

Haworth

Where are the very stones that Milton trod
— Robert Leighton, 'London'

This is no ordinary village street.
Tenacious, it holds to the hillside;
clings tight with its shops and houses.

At the top, a church, an old parsonage,
a trodden path, and beyond, the moors
which embed this place then spread for miles.

There are weathered stones under the trees
in the graveyard, for children killed by cholera,
a ramshackle arrangement, with crows stalking.

It's late afternoon and darkening.
Tourists step between the tombstones
exclaiming in their own exotic language.

and there are cobbles here in the street,
the very stone trod by the sisters' boots,
as they swished along in wide Victorian skirts,

dreaming up wild emotions and other worlds.
There's a heavy cloud looming over the moor.
And now the first fat splashing drops of rain.

Undercliffe

A white moth
has settled
on a swaying
blade of grass
on the grave
of William Greenhough
(and Elizabeth his wife).
A magpie
on an obelisk
is warning all comers.

There's a wasp
weaving a path
between the bellbind leaves
that trail from William's grave
half over Amy Wilson's
next door
(also Horace her son –
and Albert, Loving Husband
of the Above).

The Speights are here
and the Duffys,
the Whiteheads, the Cowgalls,
the Hardcastles,
all the neighbours,
all orderly, all quiet,
safe under the wings
of the cracked
stone guardians,

except that inexorably
below the earth,
the purposeful bellbind
webs the space
between William
and Amy –
mischievously
decorates their tombs
with succulent stems,
green leaves,
and with soft white trumpets.

Galleries

1.

Obviously it's winter. You're in a duffel coat,
which hides your shape. I'm lighting your fag.
There's something touching about the way we stand,
our young bodies, you leaning toward me.
We're outside the Angel Café. I'm turned away
from the camera, a back, a raised arm, a hand
holding a lit match: but you can tell it's me.

Someone says, black and white, you can't beat it.
Look at those paving stones. You can almost feel
that dusk. It's superb. Look at that lettering. I loiter
near 'Angel Lane Couple', hoping to be recognised.
But they're more interested in the dusk. The figures
make it, someone says. And I suppose we did.

2.
(Me Myself and MRI)

A slow small
carousel,
a fair
ground
where dreams may wander.

I stare
into your mind
and see only mine,
a tentative stanza
is made.

Saltaire Festival

1.

The ghost
    dances alone
on a deserted stage,
    stepping, gesturing.

His body flows
    like water round a stone;
his garments signal
    like flags in a wind.

The pole dancers
    have gone home;
paint is flaking
    from the backdrops.

Even the rear wall
    isn't real;
there's a rip
    in the canvas,

and through it I can see
    an unlit ghost
dancing with his own
    reluctant shadow.

2.

Everything is blue
in the Artist's House.

the rabbit who serves the food
is blue.
Blue stairs, blue windows.

The visitors are blue.
They wear blue clothing
blue hats – one tall, one short.

Upstairs in the blue studio
the artist paints blue pictures
under a blue tiled roof.

There is a white screen
but look. Look.
Even that is blue.

    3.

The flautist plays to the pyramids.
Although they hear the music
they don't listen.
The Sphinx, tired of his endless watch,
takes in the thin flute music.

The flautist is playing
a polyrhythmic melody
in the mixolydian mode,
but the pyramids, foursquare on their bases
are impervious to this.

They are trying to outlast time,
while the flautist is merely attempting
to ease it on its way.
Is it possible, I wonder,
that the melody will outlast the pyramids.

The Sphinx says nothing.

Joan Armatrading at St. George's Hall

Joan Armatrading at St.George's Hall,
and we are in front stalls with the fans
(having sneaked downstairs in the interval).
Joan takes the mike in eloquent dark hands,
begins her first song, cool, restrained. Guitars,
percussion, keyboards ride along with her.
The songs change: some are sweet, some quirky. There's
that swift staccato burst, that soaring slur
that lifts a high note on an endless breath;
then schmaltzy strings, then energy again.
You've had a mournful year. Your father's death
was hard. Your grief was laced with physical pain.
And there were other anguishes. But now,
just now, we live these songs, my arm round you.

My arm round you because I want it so,
because I love you, and because the music,
which knows all that a human needs to know,
tells me I should; the sound and not the lyric
guides my action. All the world is rhythmic.
A cellist throbs. A fiddler plies her bow.
Joan sings. The hall's charged with emotive static.
Music hath charms. I put my arm round you.
The tenuous spell is broken by applause
and whistling and whooping, and the beat
alters again, fierce now. And there are wars
outside this hall, and anger on the street,
and there is very little I can do.
Because I can, I put my arm round you.

Bradford Brevities, 1

Like sharpened pencils
writing on the sky's paper
the lit Christmas trees.

Look, my friend, fireworks –
a flying arc of green stars.
Wedding in the street.

Even a mile out
you hear the City Hall clock
bang out sweet music.

Ever-changing lights
at the end of Market Street
a great turning wheel.

One man who rolls dough,
marvellous exotic smells,
flames leap from the pan.

Bradford Brevities, 2

Fagley

Guy sits
in a nest of sticks.
His face is a mask.

Haworth

Tourists with pamphlets,
grey church, graves of Victorian children.
Where living children run and shout.

Kirkgate

Big Issue seller, ranter, cop,
gang of lads, wheelchair, buggie,
busker singing 'Imagine'.

Baildon

By red nasturtiums, butterflies
like flickering from a silent film,
flying snips of clean white paper.

Skyline

Grey stone spires. Towers.
Gold domes against a cloudless sky.
Tall grimed chimneys…. but no smoke.

Chosen

Many are the precious things
still hidden deep under the earth.

Many are the truths still unknown;
there are stars, galaxies never yet seen.

Many are the songs and anthems still unheard;
the poems, the mysteries are not yet complete.

None knows how many alphabets come before A,
which, still unwritten, can not be read.

Anjum KHiyali

English version by Gerard Benson
With help from Sifar Alavi and the Rev. Dominic Mughal

Rubai for Mr Hafeez Johar
(Librarian, poet and friend)

He was a man who wrote with skill and ease.
A quiet soul, who sought only for Peace.
Now he is gone, and leaves the world the poorer.
And I lament the passing of Hafeez.

I, too, can write a Ghazal if I try

I, too, can write a ghazal if I try.
I'll choose my subject and away I'll fly.

I don't believe it's all that hard to do;
I, too, can write a ghazal if I try.

But I shall choose my subject with great care.
I could write praising Earth and Sea and Sky;

I've done such things before – I can again;
Or pour down blessings on the butterfly

That flutters in my garden; or the birds.
I must write one at least before I die.

One ghazal, nicely made in every part,
To show my art with no word of a lie.

Suppose I wrote of Bradford, where I live?
Or London, where I used to live? Or Rye,

that curious Kentish town where some years past
we spent some happy days, Cathy and I?

That would be nice to do, or I could pen
A charming song – a little lullaby.

(If I did that, the audience might sleep
And that would be a shame) I'll prophesy!

That's what I'll do, telling it like it is.
My verse will change the world, from low to high;

And yet that's not my style. It's not my way.
I'll think of something else. Supposing I

Wrote a few lines fit for a summer night,
An evening in June or in July.

And read them, wearing shirt and jazzy tie,
To make the people smile, not make them cry –

Just write the verse and never question why.
Yes, I can write a ghazal, if I try.

Garlic

The back door faces north. The pail I left
in the rain has forged a hoop of dirty ice,
dry and hard as iron. The air's a vice
that clamps the ribs and almost stops the breath.
I'm planting garlic. Soil, forked over only
yesterday, is rigid now, the spade strikes
and sings aloud, as though I had hit stone.
With cold red fingers I tamp in the moonlike
cloves, carefully set them in fresh compost
from my heap, which, even in this freezing
season, is warm and sweet. I chop with my trowel
at lumps, trying to form a tilth; kneeling
in white rime I imagine summer's tossed
lettuce, endives, capers – vinegar, olive oil.

Winter Stew

Chopped leeks, shallots, and onions cut in slices,
salt, pepper, basil and assorted spices,
an ounce or two of butter (oil will do)
will serve to start this warming winter stew.
Heat these together, moving them around;
make certain that the onions are not browned.
Add just a touch of stock and raise the heat
a notch or two. Now you should add the meat:
inch cubes of first rate beef or lamb
coated in flour; (a slice of good lean ham
or thickish bacon adds a piquant touch).
Pour in some rich beef stock, but not too much,
and stir. Bring to the boil and add the veg –
potatoes, two small chillis (which give edge),
carrots, a head of garlic, both cut fine;
stew for one hour and serve with rough red wine.

So Snow

I've felt the earth in the garden harden,
and seen the traffic at a standstill till
the council lorry came and the grit bit.
I sit inside, my hands round a snug mug
and watch the quarry on this high hill fill
with drifting snow till its bright white
dazzles me. I watch my neighbour labour
to clear his path, then see him trudge, sludge
up to his ankles, to the *North Star* bar
to spend his pension and some gin and lime time
with the barman. The radio forecast is for more
of the same. And now as I look up at the sky I
shudder, watching a black cloud shroud
the dales. It's miserable. I'm miserable. Enough said. Bed.

Eclipse

Someone
    took a bite out of the moon
Someone
    pulled a curtain of blood
        over her eye

If I Hadn't Been a Writer

If I hadn't been a writer,
  I might have been a vet,
or then again I might ha'
  played the drums in a Quintet,
been a plumber in the summer
  when the weather's nice and hot,
and a printer in the winter
  to be indoors when it's not.

I might have been a dancer
  (no, not a ballerina
but a tapdance fancy-pantser).
  I have been a window-cleaner;
or I could have been a waiter
  or at least a washer-upper,
or the bloke behind the counter
  who serves you with your cuppa.

A postman, a bricklayer,
  or a boxer or a ref,
or a pub piano-player,
  or a butcher or a chef.
Or a barber or hair-dresser,
  A caretaker or teacher
or even a professor,
  or, at a pinch, a preacher.

But I might be something quiet,
  a librarian perhaps,
an adviser about diet,
  an expert on old maps;
or something with adventures,
  a stunt man (that's exciting!)
and catch bullets in my dentures...
  No! I think I'll stick to writing.

How Delightful To Know Mr Benson

How delightful to know Mr Benson
everyone wants to know him –
so witty and charming and handsome
(Though some think he's ugly and dim).

His quips never verge on the personal,
though sometimes he puns people's names.
He's a lifelong supporter of Arsenal
though it's years since he went to their games.

He moved up to Yorkshire from Highbury
to devote extra time to his rhymes,
and he lives in a sort of a library,
and tends a small garden, sometimes.

He hasn't been made Poet Laureate.
His face hasn't been in *Hello!*
(Two facts that he's not all that sorry at)
but, (ah!) he's delightful to know.

❋

But now that he *is* Poet Laureate
of Bradford, that excellent city,
he finds that it's nothing to worry at,
it's an honour. And so ends my ditty.

NB: The first verses were written some time ago and have appeared in the *New Statesman* and in Gerard's children's collection, *Omba Bolomba*. The coda was written after he'd accepted the role of Poet Laureate for Bradford. The whole piece is based on Edward Lear's 'How Pleasant to Know Mr. Lear'.

Community Pride

We're a city of variety: of churches, mosques and chapels,
synagogues, meeting houses, temples and tabernacles,
   (put them in any order you like).
I take pride in our variety – but it's pride in the people,
not pride in dome, roof, tower or steeple.
   I'm proud of the pram- pusher, the kid on his first bike,
the ambulance driver, the stroller. We're a diverse city;
various and proud of it. That's the nitty- gritty.
   But it's not people's beliefs, it's how they act;
that's where our pride can reside. It's when we gather,
show concerns, befriend one another, do things together,
   greet our neighbours in the street; use a little tact,
accepting differences and embracing similarities.
We come from many backgrounds and many countries,
   Wear clothes of multifarious styles; cloth cap, prayer cap;
fashion boot, Doc Martens, trainers; saree, shalwar kameez,
kanga, shirt, skirt and blouse; jeans, track suit, three piece.
   But it's the people, not their clothes. People. The chap
I call The Illustrated Lad, tattooed with a horrible dragon
giving up his seat on the bus to a pregnant woman.
   It's the people – and the places where we meet;
market, park, school, sports centre, museum, art gallery,
cinema, bench, playing field. We become a community
     when we come out of our houses and meet in the street.